Preface

Welcome to **Discovering Machine Learning: A Gentle Introduction to AI**. This book is designed to help you understand the basics and applications of machine learning, a field that is changing the way we use technology.

This book covers a wide range of topics to give you a solid foundation in machine learning. We start with basic concepts and gradually move to more advanced topics. You will learn about supervised learning, unsupervised learning, reinforcement learning, and how to evaluate models.

Whether you are a student, a professional, or just curious about machine learning, this book is for you. By the end, you will have the knowledge and skills to create your own machine learning models and understand how they work.

We hope this book makes the world of machine learning accessible and exciting for you.

Happy learning!

Contents

What is Machine Learning

In simple terms, Machine Learning means a **Machine that learns**.

Machine Learning is a branch of **Artificial Intelligence** which focuses on enabling computers to perform tasks based on data and with minimal human interference.

I should make it clear that the aim of Machine Learning is to build intelligent systems which can learn from data, identify patterns and make decisions to help humans; not to replace them. **Nothing can replace humans.**

Above description and definition of Machine Learning is for non-technical people who doesn't want to build career in this Area.

Let's discuss Machine with an intention to build a career out of it.

Before understanding Machine learning we should answer what it is learning.

Learning is the ability to improve one's behavior with experience. It means learning is a continuous process of doing a task, evaluating the result of that task, improving based on the result, and doing the task again in a better and more efficient way.

For example, A marathon runner runs for a couple of miles, evaluates his performance, works on his performance and runs again.

Now, what is Machine Learning?

Machine learning is the study of computer algorithms that learns and builds models from data. These models can be used for prediction, decision making or solving tasks.

A computer algorithm is said to learn from experience E with respect to some class of tasks T and performance measure P if it's performance of tasks T as measured by P improves with experience E.

Difference between Traditional Programming and Machine Learning

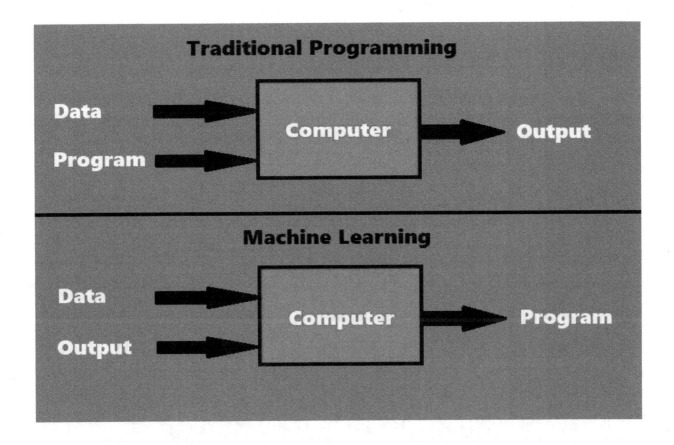

In traditional programming a programmer or a user writes a piece of code or program and input data into a computer to get a result or Output; whereas in Machine learning user must supply computer with Data and output, the computer then builds a Model or Program to increase the efficiency and accuracy of the task.

Suppose we take an example of a Credit Card system, by using traditional programming we can get information like who is paying the bills on time and who is not, but if we apply Machine Learning; we can use data such as income, expenditure, demography etc. to determine whether the person will or will not pay the bill on time.

Architecture of Machine Learning

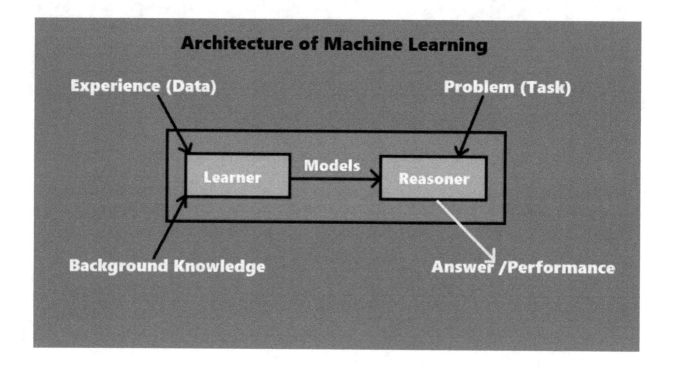

If we consider Machine learning system as a box, there are two main components in it:

- **Learner**

- **Reasoner**

Learner takes Experience and Background knowledge to build Model; this model can be used by the Reasoner to find a solution of a task provided to it.

Types of Machine Learning

There are mainly three ways in which a Machine learns:

1. **Supervised Learning:** Model learns from labeled examples to make predictions or decisions.

2. **Unsupervised Learning:** Model finds patterns and relationships in data without labeled examples.

3. **Reinforcement Learning:** An agent learns by taking actions in an environment to maximize rewards.

We will discuss types of Machine Learning in detail in the next chapters.

AI Vs ML

In today's tech-driven world, terms like **Artificial Intelligence** (AI) and **Machine Learning** (ML) are often used interchangeably, leading to confusion about their actual meanings and applications. However, it's crucial to recognize that while AI and ML are closely related, they serve distinct purposes and operate in different ways.

At its core, **Artificial Intelligence** refers to the simulation of human intelligence in machines, enabling them to perform tasks that typically require human intelligence, such as learning, problem-solving, perception, and decision-making. AI encompasses a broad spectrum of capabilities, ranging from simple rule-based systems to complex autonomous machines capable of reasoning and self-improvement.

On the other hand, **Machine Learning** is a subset of AI that focuses on the development of algorithms that allow computers to learn from and make predictions or decisions based on data, without being explicitly programmed to perform specific tasks. In essence, ML algorithms learn from historical data patterns and iteratively improve their performance over time, making them increasingly accurate and effective at their designated tasks.

To illustrate the difference between AI and ML, consider the analogy of a self-driving car. The AI component encompasses the overall system's ability to perceive its environment, navigate roads, and make decisions in real-time, akin to human intelligence. Within this AI framework, Machine Learning algorithms play a crucial role in tasks like recognizing traffic signs, predicting pedestrian behavior, and optimizing driving routes based on historical traffic data.

In summary, while AI represents the broader concept of imbuing machines with human-like intelligence, Machine Learning serves as a specific approach within the AI domain, focusing on algorithms that enable computers to learn from data and improve their performance over time. Understanding this distinction is essential for grasping the diverse applications and potential implications of these transformative technologies in various fields, from healthcare and finance to transportation and beyond.

Supervised Learning

We discussed Machine learning in the first chapter. Now let's discuss Supervised Learning; the most common and widely used branch of Machine Learning.

Suppose you are a student who wants to learn a new language, you will need a teacher who can teach you different words of that language and their meaning. Once you understand and memorize these words, you can form a sentence and finally be able to speak and write in that language. This entire learning occurred under the Supervision of that teacher, so you can say that it was a Supervised learning.

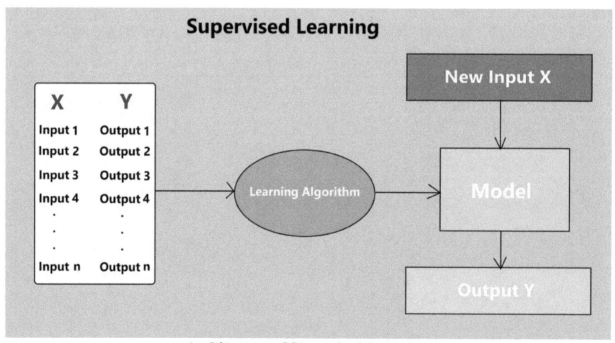

Architecture of Supervised Learning

Similarly, in Supervised Machine learning, set of instances are provided to the learning Algorithm, each instance contains an input and an output. The Algorithm learns from these instances and builds a model which can then find output to any new input.

In Supervised learning, you show the machine the connection between different variables and known outcomes. This is called Labeled data and Sample output. Therefore, you can also say that **Supervised learning is Learning with Labeled Data.**

Suppose you want to build a program which can identify different types of vehicles on the road, in order to train the algorithm, you need to feed images of different vehicles to it and assign labels to those images, for example you upload images of different cars and tag them as Cars. This process is called Training the algorithm. After training completes, the time for Testing the Algorithm arrives; during Testing, we upload images of a random vehicle without assigning any tags to them. The algorithm then analyzes each image and assigns a tag to it, if the tag is correct then training has been successful, and the Machine has learned.

There are many algorithms used in Supervised Learning, they can be broadly categorized into two categories:

1. Classification

2. Regression

We will discuss both in the next chapter.

Classification Algorithms

Classification is a predictive modeling task where the output variable is a category. The input features can be continuous or categorical, but the output is always categorical. Some common examples of classification tasks include:

- Email spam detection (spam or not spam)
- Image recognition (classifying images into categories like cats, dogs, etc.)
- Medical diagnosis (diseases based on symptoms)

Types of Classification Algorithms

Several classification algorithms are commonly used in supervised learning, each with unique characteristics. Here, we discuss some of the most widely used ones.

1. Logistic Regression

Logistic regression is a statistical model that in its basic form uses a logistic function to model a binary dependent variable. Despite its name, it is a classification algorithm.

Principle:

Logistic regression estimates the probability that an instance belongs to a particular class. It uses the logistic function (sigmoid) to squeeze the output of a linear equation between 0 and 1.

Equation:

$\sigma(z) = 1/(1+e^{-z})$

where $z = \beta_0 + \beta_1 x_1 + \beta_2 x_2 + \cdots + \beta_n x_n$

Strengths:

- Easy to implement and interpret.
- Effective for linearly separable data.
- Provides probabilities for class membership.

Weaknesses:

- Assumes a linear relationship between the input features and the log odds.
- Can struggle with complex, non-linear relationships.

Applications:

- Binary classification problems such as spam detection and credit scoring.

2. Decision Trees

Decision trees are a non-parametric supervised learning method used for classification and regression. They predict the value of a target variable by learning simple decision rules inferred from the data features.

Principle:

A decision tree splits the data into subsets based on the value of input features. This process is repeated recursively, creating a tree-like model of decisions.

Key Components:

- **Nodes:** Represent a feature or attribute.
- **Edges:** Represent the outcome of a decision.
- **Leaves:** Represent the final output or class.

Strengths:

- Easy to understand and interpret.
- Can handle both numerical and categorical data.
- Requires little data preprocessing.

Weaknesses:

- Prone to overfitting.
- Can create biased trees if some classes dominate.

Applications:

- Customer segmentation.
- Credit risk assessment.

3. Random Forest

Random forest is an ensemble learning method that operates by constructing a multitude of decision trees during training and outputting the class that is the mode of the classes (classification) of the individual trees.

Principle:

Random forests combine the predictions of multiple decision trees to improve generalization and reduce overfitting.

Key Components:

- **Ensemble of Trees:** Multiple decision trees are created using bootstrapped subsets of the data.
- **Random Feature Selection:** At each split, a random subset of features is chosen to determine the best split.

Strengths:

- Reduces overfitting compared to individual decision trees.
- Handles large datasets with higher dimensionality.
- Provides feature importance.

Weaknesses:

- Can be slower and more complex to interpret.
- Requires more computational resources.

Applications:

- Medical diagnosis.
- Stock market prediction.

4. Support Vector Machines (SVM)

Support vector machines are supervised learning models used for classification and regression analysis. They are effective in high-dimensional spaces and for cases where the number of dimensions exceeds the number of samples.

Principle:

SVMs find a hyperplane that best divides a dataset into classes. The hyperplane was chosen to maximize the margin between the classes.

Key Components:

- **Hyperplane:** The decision boundary that separates different classes.
- **Support Vectors:** The data points that are closest to the hyperplane and influence its position.

Strengths:

- Effective in high-dimensional spaces.
- Robust to overfitting, especially in high-dimensional space.
- Works well for both linear and non-linear classification (with kernel trick).

Weaknesses:

- Can be memory-intensive and computationally expensive.
- Harder to interpret the final model.

Applications:

- Image classification.
- Text categorization.

5. k-Nearest Neighbors (k-NN)

k-Nearest Neighbors is a simple, instance-based learning algorithm where the classification of a data point is based on the majority class among its k nearest neighbors.

Principle:

The algorithm assigns the class of a data point based on the classes of the k nearest data points in the feature space.

Key Components:

- **Distance Metric:** Typically, Euclidean distance, but other distance metrics can be used.
- **k Value:** The number of neighbors to consider.

Strengths:

- Simple and easy to implement.
- No training phase required.
- Naturally handles multi-class classification.

Weaknesses:

- Computationally expensive during prediction.
- Performance degrades with high-dimensional data.

Applications:

- Recommender systems.
- Anomaly detection.

Conclusion

Classification algorithms are fundamental to supervised learning, each with unique strengths and suitable applications. Selecting the right algorithm depends on the specific problem, dataset characteristics, and performance requirements. Understanding the principles, strengths, and weaknesses of each method enables practitioners to make informed choices and build effective predictive models.

Future advancements in classification techniques and the development of more sophisticated ensemble methods promise to further enhance the accuracy and applicability of these models in various domains.

Regression Algorithms

Regression is a type of supervised learning where the goal is to predict a continuous target variable based on input features.

Regression involves predicting a numeric value, unlike classification, which predicts categorical outcomes. Common regression tasks include:

- Predicting house prices based on features like size, location, and age.
- Estimating a person's weight based on height and age.

Types of Regression Algorithms

1. Linear Regression

Linear regression models the relationship between a dependent variable and one or more independent variables using a linear equation.

Principle:

The model fits a line to the data by minimizing the sum of squared differences between observed and predicted values.

Equation:

$$y = \beta_0 + \beta_1 x_1 + \beta_2 x_2 + \cdots + \beta_n x_n$$

Strengths:

- Simple to implement and interpret.
- Efficient for small to medium-sized datasets.

Weaknesses:

- Assumes a linear relationship.
- Sensitive to outliers.

Applications:

- Predicting sales.
- Estimating economic indicators.

2. Polynomial Regression

Polynomial regression models the relationship between the independent variable and the dependent variable as an nth degree polynomial.

Principle:

Transforms input features into polynomial features of a given degree.

Equation:

$$y=\beta_0+\beta_1x+\beta_2x^2+\cdots+\beta_nx^n$$

Strengths:

- Captures non-linear relationships.

Weaknesses:

- Prone to overfitting with high-degree polynomials.
- Can be complex to interpret.

Applications:

- Modeling growth rates.
- Predicting trends.

3. Decision Tree Regression

Decision tree regression splits the data into subsets based on feature values and fits a simple model within each subset.

Principle:

Recursive binary splitting creates a tree where each leaf represents a prediction.

Strengths:

- Handles non-linear relationships well.
- Easy to interpret visually.

Weaknesses:

- Can overfit if the tree is too deep.
- Sensitive to small changes in data.

Applications:

- Stock price prediction.
- Forecasting.

4. Random Forest Regression

Random forest regression uses multiple decision trees to improve prediction accuracy.

Principle:

Combines predictions from many trees, each trained on a random subset of data.

Strengths:

- Reduces overfitting compared to single decision trees.
- Handles large datasets well.

Weaknesses:

- More computationally intensive.
- Less interpretable than individual decision trees.

Applications:

- Predicting loan defaults.
- Analyzing complex datasets.

5. Support Vector Regression (SVR)

SVR extends support vector machines to predict continuous values, using a margin of tolerance.

Principle:

Finds a function that deviates from actual observations by a value no greater than a specified margin.

Strengths:

- Effective in high-dimensional spaces.
- Robust to outliers.

Weaknesses:

- Requires careful tuning of parameters.
- Computationally expensive.

Applications:

- Financial forecasting.
- Time series prediction.

6. k-Nearest Neighbors Regression (k-NN)

k-NN regression predicts a value based on the average of the k nearest neighbors.

Principle:

Uses distance metrics to find the closest data points in the feature space.

Strengths:

- Simple and intuitive.
- No training phase.

Weaknesses:

- Computationally expensive for large datasets.
- Performance degrades with high-dimensional data.

Applications:

- Estimating property values.
- Predicting customer behavior.

Conclusion

Regression algorithms are vital for predicting continuous outcomes. Selecting the right algorithm depends on the problem at hand and data characteristics. Understanding these algorithms helps build effective models, ensuring accurate predictions and insights. Future developments in regression techniques will likely enhance their applicability and performance in various fields.

UnSupervised Learning

The basic idea of Unsupervised Learning is to feed machines with as much data as possible without providing any label on the data and letting machine group similar data together to form clusters and provide insights on them.

In Unsupervised Learning, the learning algorithm tries to understand relationships between various inputs without any pre-existing information.

In other words, there are only inputs present and the learning algorithm groups them into clusters.

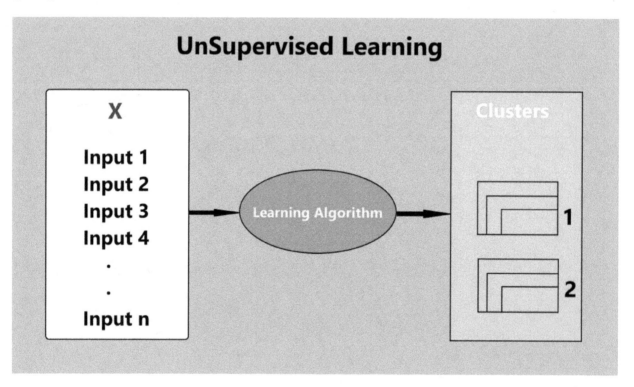

Let's take an example. Suppose you are visiting a religious site of a religion other than yours. I am sure it will be difficult for you to understand and perform different rituals being performed, what do you do in that case?

First you start to notice people around you:

Are they folding their hands, if yes then how?

Are they moving in a certain direction?

Are they chanting something?

What kind of clothes did they wear?

Are they offering something to the idol?

And many other questions.

At certain point you will have a basic understanding of what to do after watching people around you, you may still not know what those rituals mean but you will be able to perform those rituals.

The same thing happens with the machine, the machine takes the data, groups similar data together without knowing what they mean, and we use these groups to get insights.

Unsupervised learning has many practical applications such as:

- To group Customers based on their purchase history.
- To group patients together based on their conditions.

One of the biggest benefits of Unsupervised learning is that you can get patterns or insights which you didn't expect at all and could never have gotten from Supervised learning.

Question: What happens when we use Supervised learning and Unsupervised learning together?

Answer: We get Semi- Supervised Learning.

Semi- Supervised Learning is a combination of Supervised Learning and Unsupervised Learning. It means the Machine get a large amount of unlabeled data along with a small amount of labelled data. This learning helps us in getting insights on known indicators as well as on unknown ones, if any.

UnSupervised Learning algorithms can be broadly categorized into two categories:

1. Clustering
2. Dimensionality reduction

Clustering Algorithms

Clustering involves identifying and grouping similar data points in a dataset without predefined labels. It's widely used for data analysis, pattern recognition, and information retrieval. Common clustering tasks include:

- Customer segmentation in marketing.
- Document clustering in information retrieval.
- Image segmentation in computer vision.

Types of Clustering Algorithms

1. k-Means Clustering

k-Means clustering partitions the dataset into k clusters, with each data point belonging to the cluster with the nearest mean.

Principle:

The algorithm iteratively assigns data points to clusters based on the closest mean and then updates the means based on the current assignments.

Steps:

1. Initialize k centroids randomly.

2. Assign each data point to the nearest centroid.

3. Recalculate the centroids as the mean of the assigned points.

4. Repeat steps 2 and 3 until convergence.

Strengths:

- Simple and fast for large datasets.
- Easy to implement.

Weaknesses:

- Requires the number of clusters (k) to be specified.
- Sensitive to initial centroid placement.
- Assumes spherical clusters.

Applications:

- Market segmentation.
- Image compression.

2. Hierarchical Clustering

Hierarchical clustering builds a hierarchy of clusters either through a bottom-up (agglomerative) or top-down (divisive) approach.

Principle:

- **Agglomerative:** Starts with each data point as a single cluster and merges the closest pairs of clusters iteratively.
- **Divisive:** Starts with one cluster and recursively splits it into smaller clusters.

Steps (Agglomerative):

1. Compute the distance matrix.

2. Merge the closest pair of clusters.

3. Update the distance matrix.

4. Repeat steps 2 and 3 until only one cluster remains.

Strengths:

- No need to specify the number of clusters.
- Produces a dendrogram for easy visualization.

Weaknesses:

- Computationally intensive for large datasets.
- Sensitive to noise and outliers.

Applications:

- Gene expression analysis.
- Document clustering.

3. DBSCAN (Density-Based Spatial Clustering of Applications with Noise)

DBSCAN identifies clusters based on the density of data points, making it effective for discovering clusters of arbitrary shape.

Principle:

The algorithm defines clusters as areas of high density separated by areas of low density. Points in low-density areas are marked as noise.

Key Parameters:

- **Epsilon (ε):** The radius within which to search for neighboring points.
- **MinPts:** The minimum number of points required to form a dense region.

Steps:

1. Identify core points that have at least MinPts within ε.

2. Expand clusters from core points.

3. Mark points that are not reachable from any core point as noise.

Strengths:

- Does not require the number of clusters to be specified.
- Can find arbitrarily shaped clusters.
- Handles noise effectively.

Weaknesses:

- Sensitive to the choice of ε and MinPts.
- Struggles with varying densities.

Applications:

- Geographic data analysis.
- Anomaly detection.

4. Mean Shift Clustering

Mean Shift is a centroid-based algorithm that updates centroids to the mean of points within a given radius until convergence.

Principle:

The algorithm shifts centroids towards the highest density of data points iteratively.

Steps:

1. Initialize centroids randomly.

2. For each centroid, compute the mean of points within a radius.

3. Shift the centroid to the mean.

4. Repeat until convergence.

Strengths:

- Does not require specifying the number of clusters.
- Can find arbitrarily shaped clusters.

Weaknesses:

- Computationally expensive for large datasets.
- Choice of bandwidth parameter can be challenging.

Applications:

- Image segmentation.
- Object tracking.

5. Gaussian Mixture Models (GMM)

GMM assumes that the data is generated from a mixture of several Gaussian distributions with unknown parameters.

Principle:

The algorithm uses the Expectation-Maximization (EM) algorithm to estimate the parameters of the Gaussian distributions.

Steps:

1. Initialize the parameters (means, covariances, and mixing coefficients).

2. E-step: Calculate the probability that each point belongs to each Gaussian.

3. M-step: Update the parameters based on the probabilities.

4. Repeat steps 2 and 3 until convergence.

Strengths:

- Can model clusters with different shapes and sizes.
- Provides a probabilistic clustering approach.

Weaknesses:

- Requires specifying the number of clusters.
- Sensitive to initialization.

Applications:

- Speaker recognition.
- Image segmentation.

Conclusion

Clustering algorithms are fundamental to unsupervised learning, enabling the discovery of hidden patterns in data. Each algorithm has unique strengths and is suitable for different types of data and applications. Understanding these algorithms allows practitioners to choose the right approach for their specific problem, ensuring effective clustering and valuable insights. Future advancements will continue to enhance clustering techniques, making them more robust, scalable, and adaptable to various domains.

Dimensionality Reduction Algorithms

High-dimensional data can lead to several challenges, such as increased computational cost, overfitting, and difficulty in visualization. Dimensionality reduction addresses these issues by transforming data into a lower-dimensional space. Key benefits include:

- **Reduced Computational Cost:** Lower-dimensional data requires less computational power.
- **Improved Model Performance:** Reducing dimensions can help prevent overfitting.
- **Enhanced Visualization:** Data in two or three dimensions can be visualized more easily.

Types of Dimensionality Reduction Techniques

1. Principal Component Analysis (PCA)

PCA is a linear technique that transforms the data into a new coordinate system where the greatest variances are represented by new axes (principal components).

Principle:

PCA identifies the directions (principal components) along which the variance of the data is maximized.

Steps:

1. Standardize the data.

2. Compute the covariance matrix.

3. Calculate the eigenvalues and eigenvectors of the covariance matrix.

4. Sort the eigenvectors by decreasing eigenvalues and select the top k.

5. Transform the original data using the top k eigenvectors.

Strengths:

- Reduces dimensions while retaining most variance.
- Efficient and easy to implement.

Weaknesses:

- Assumes linear relationships.
- Sensitive to outliers.

Applications:

- Image compression.
- Exploratory data analysis.

2. Linear Discriminant Analysis (LDA)

LDA is a supervised technique used for dimensionality reduction while preserving the class discriminatory information.

Principle:

LDA maximizes the ratio of between-class variance to within-class variance in the data.

Steps:

1. Compute the within-class and between-class scatter matrices.

2. Calculate the eigenvalues and eigenvectors for the scatter matrices.

3. Select the top k eigenvectors based on the largest eigenvalues.

4. Transform the data using these eigenvectors.

Strengths:

- Improves class separability.
- Useful for classification tasks.

Weaknesses:

- Assumes normally distributed classes with identical covariances.
- Not suitable for unsupervised tasks.

Applications:

- Face recognition.
- Pattern recognition.

3. t-Distributed Stochastic Neighbor Embedding (t-SNE)

t-SNE is a non-linear technique primarily used for visualizing high-dimensional data in two or three dimensions.

Principle:

t-SNE minimizes the divergence between two distributions: one representing pairwise similarities in the high-dimensional space and the other in the low-dimensional space.

Steps:

1. Compute pairwise similarities in high-dimensional space.

2. Compute pairwise similarities in low-dimensional space.

3. Minimize the Kullback-Leibler divergence between these distributions using gradient descent.

Strengths:

- Excellent for visualization.
- Captures complex structures in data.

Weaknesses:

- Computationally intensive.
- Not suitable for large datasets.

Applications:

- Visualizing clusters.
- Exploring high-dimensional biological data.

4. Uniform Manifold Approximation and Projection (UMAP)

UMAP is a non-linear technique used for dimensionality reduction and visualization, similar to t-SNE but more efficient.

Principle:

UMAP constructs a high-dimensional graph of the data and then optimizes a low-dimensional graph to be as structurally similar as possible.

Steps:

1. Construct a fuzzy topological representation of the data.

2. Optimize the low-dimensional representation to preserve the topological structure.

Strengths:

- Faster and more scalable than t-SNE.
- Preserves more of the global data structure.

Weaknesses:

- Hyperparameter tuning can be complex.
- Interpretation of the embedding can be challenging.

Applications:

- Visualizing large datasets.
- Analyzing high-dimensional data in bioinformatics.

5. Autoencoders

Autoencoders are neural networks used for learning efficient codings of input data for dimensionality reduction.

Principle:

An autoencoder consists of an encoder that compresses the input data and a decoder that reconstructs the original data from the compressed representation.

Steps:

1. Train the autoencoder on the input data.

2. Use the encoder part to transform data into a lower-dimensional space.

3. Optionally use the decoder to reconstruct the data for evaluation.

Strengths:

- Capable of capturing non-linear relationships.
- Can handle large and complex datasets.

Weaknesses:

- Requires substantial computational resources.
- Training can be challenging.

Applications:

- Image and speech processing.
- Anomaly detection.

Conclusion

Dimensionality reduction is a crucial step in preprocessing high-dimensional data, enhancing computational efficiency, and improving model performance. Selecting the right technique depends on the nature of the data and the specific application. Understanding these techniques enables practitioners to reduce dimensionality effectively, ensuring that valuable information is retained while simplifying the dataset. Future advancements in this field will continue to improve the scalability and applicability of dimensionality reduction methods across various domains.

Reinforcement Learning

Reinforcement Learning is an area of Machine Learning which is applied when you don't have training dataset and want the machine to learn from its experience.

How Reinforcement Learning works:

Step1: A problem is given to the Computer or Agent.

Step 2: The Agent uses trial and error method to find a solution for the given problem.

Step 3: The Agent gets either rewards or penalties from the environment for the actions it performs.

Step 4: The Agent learns from the reward and tries again to find the solution of the problem.

Step 5: Step 2 to Step 4 goes on for several loops or iterations.

Step 6: Agent's goal is to maximize the total reward.

Reinforcement Learning

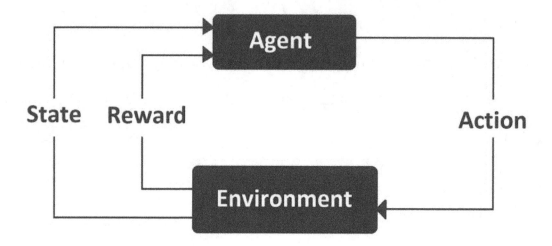

Difference between Supervised and Reinforcement learning:

Supervised learning uses the correct set of output as feedback for performing a task whereas Reinforcement learning uses rewards and punishment as feedback for the actions performed to find the solution.

Difference between Unsupervised and Reinforcement learning:

The goal in Unsupervised learning is to find similarities and differences between data points whereas the goal in Reinforcement learning is to find a suitable action model that would maximize the total cumulative reward of the agent.

Applications of Reinforcement Learning:

Reinforcement Learning is and cab be widely used in the following sectors:

- Gaming
- Robotics
- Industrial Operations
- Supply Chain & Logistics
- Traffic Control
- Bidding & Advertising
- Augmented Natural Language Processing (NLP)

Types of Reinforcement Learning Algorithms

- Model-Free Algorithms

- Model-Based Algorithms

We will discuss them in the next chapter.

Model-Free Algorithms

Model-free algorithms do not require a model of the environment and learn policies directly from interaction with the environment. They can be further divided into value-based methods and policy-based methods.

Value-Based Methods

Q-Learning

Q-Learning is a value-based method where the agent learns the value of state-action pairs (Q-values) and uses these values to select actions.

Principle:

The Q-value of a state-action pair is updated using the Bellman equation:

$$Q(s,a) \leftarrow Q(s,a) + \alpha[r + \gamma \max a' Q(s',a') - Q(s,a)]$$

Strengths:

- Simple to implement.
- Converges to the optimal policy given sufficient exploration.

Weaknesses:

- Inefficient for large state spaces.
- Requires a discrete action space.

Applications:

- Game playing (e.g., simple grid-based games).
- Robotics (simple navigation tasks).

SARSA (State-Action-Reward-State-Action)

SARSA is an on-policy value-based method similar to Q-Learning, but it updates the Q-value based on the action actually taken by the current policy.

Principle:

The Q-value update rule is:

$$Q(s,a) \leftarrow Q(s,a) + \alpha[r + \gamma Q(s',a') - Q(s,a)]$$

Strengths:

- Can be more stable than Q-Learning in some scenarios.
- Suitable for environments where the policy needs to be considered during learning.

Weaknesses:

- Also inefficient for large state spaces.

- Requires a discrete action space.

Applications:

- Game playing.

- Autonomous driving in simple simulations.

Policy-Based Methods

REINFORCE

REINFORCE is a policy gradient method that directly optimizes the policy by adjusting the policy parameters to maximize expected rewards.

Principle:

The policy parameters are updated using the gradient of the expected return:

$$\theta \leftarrow \theta + \alpha \nabla_\theta \log \pi_\theta(a|s) G_t$$

where Gt is the return following time step t.

Strengths:

- Works well with continuous action spaces.
- Directly optimizes the policy.

Weaknesses:

- High variance in gradient estimates.
- Requires careful tuning of learning rates.

Applications:

- Robotics (complex control tasks).
- Finance (portfolio management).

Actor-Critic Methods

Actor-Critic methods combine value-based and policy-based approaches, using an actor to propose actions and a critic to evaluate them.

Principle:

The actor updates the policy parameters, while the critic updates the value function, typically using Temporal Difference (TD) methods.

Strengths:

- Lower variance in gradient estimates compared to REINFORCE.
- Suitable for both discrete and continuous action spaces.

Weaknesses:

- More complex to implement and tune.
- Can be less stable without proper tuning.

Applications:

- Game playing (e.g., board games like Go).
- Robotics (manipulation tasks).

Model-Based Algorithms

Model-based algorithms use a model of the environment to simulate interactions and plan actions. They can improve sample efficiency but are often more complex to implement.

Dyna-Q

Dyna-Q is a model-based approach that integrates learning, planning, and acting by updating Q-values based on both real and simulated experiences.

Principle:

It combines Q-learning with simulated experiences generated by a learned model of the environment.

Strengths:

- More sample efficient than pure model-free methods.
- Integrates planning into the learning process.

Weaknesses:

- Requires an accurate model of the environment.
- More computationally intensive.

Applications:

- Robotics (complex navigation and manipulation tasks).
- Real-time strategy games.

Monte Carlo Tree Search (MCTS)

MCTS is a planning algorithm that uses Monte Carlo simulations to evaluate the possible future states and actions.

Principle:

It builds a search tree by simulating many random games, using the results to estimate the value of actions.

Strengths:

- Effective for environments with a large search space.
- Balances exploration and exploitation well.

Weaknesses:

- Computationally intensive.
- Requires many simulations for accurate value estimates.

Applications:

- Game playing (e.g., Chess, Go).
- Real-time decision-making (e.g., autonomous vehicles).

Simple Machine Learning Program in Python to Use Linear Regression to predict House Price.

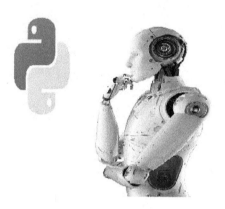

Requirement: The main requirement is to be able to assign and predict House Price in a given location based on age of house, distance from Airport and number of conveniences stores within 5 km radius.

Python IDE for Machine Learning used for the program: Google Colab

Dataset: RealEstate.xlsx (https://docs.google.com/spreadsheets/d/1rDxK1UJ8m3Vk7-3FlvP5ubm0je5f1MYF/edit?usp=drive_link&ouid=111045817766975045232&rtpof=true&sd=true)

Let's start coding:

import pandas

from sklearn.model_selection import train_test_split

from sklearn import linear_model

from matplotlib import pylab

from pylab import *

Read data and excel source and store it in Dataframe.

df = pandas.read_excel("/content/RealEstate.xlsx")

#Display the Dataframe

display(df)

```
import pandas
from sklearn.model_selection import train_test_split
from sklearn import linear_model
from matplotlib import pylab
from pylab import *

# Read data and excel source and store it in Dataframe.
df = pandas.read_excel("/content/RealEstate.xlsx")

#Display the Dataframe
display(df)
```

	No	TransactionDate	HouseAge	DistanceFromAirport	NumberOfConvenienceStores	Latitude	Longitude	HousePriceinThousands
0	1	2012.917	32.0	84.87882	10	24.98298	121.54024	37.9
1	2	2012.917	19.5	306.59470	9	24.98034	121.53951	42.2
2	3	2013.583	13.3	561.98450	5	24.98746	121.54391	47.3
3	4	2013.500	13.3	561.98450	5	24.98746	121.54391	54.8
4	5	2012.833	5.0	390.56840	5	24.97937	121.54245	43.1
...	...	...	...	...	...	...	...	...
409	410	2013.000	13.7	4082.01500	0	24.94155	121.50381	15.4
410	411	2012.667	5.6	90.45606	9	24.97433	121.54310	50.0
411	412	2013.250	18.8	390.96960	7	24.97923	121.53986	40.6
412	413	2013.000	8.1	104.81010	5	24.96674	121.54067	52.5
413	414	2013.500	6.5	90.45606	9	24.97433	121.54310	63.9

414 rows × 8 columns

Remove rows and columns with Null/NaN values.

df=df.dropna(how='any')

Since we want to predict the HousePrice based on HouseAge, DistanceFromAirport and NumberOfConvenienceStores. Remove all other columns from the Dataset.

df= df.drop(columns=['No','TransactionDate','Latitude','Longitude'])

Select the column to predict.

y=df.pop('HousePriceinThousands')

Select the columns based on which prediction will be done.

x =df.values

#Dsiplay the y value

display(y)

```
[27] # Remove rows and columns with Null/NaN values.
     df=df.dropna(how='any')

     # Since we want to predict the HousePrice based on HouseAge, DistanceFromAirport and NumberOfConvenienceStores. Remove all other columns from the Dataset.
     df= df.drop(columns=['No','TransactionDate','Latitude','Longitude'])

     # Select the column to predict.
     y=df.pop('HousePriceInThousands')

     # Select the columns based on which prediction will be done.
     x =df.values

     #Dsiplay the y value
     display(y)

     0      37.9
     1      42.2
     2      47.3
     3      54.8
     4      43.1
            ...
     409    15.4
     410    50.0
     411    40.6
     412    52.5
     413    63.9
     Name: HousePriceInThousands, Length: 414, dtype: float64
```

#Let's divide the dataset into two parts, one for training and other for testing.

x_train, x_test, y_train, y_test = train_test_split(x, y, train_size=0.33, test_size=0.67, random_state=100)

#Selecting the Algorithm for the model: Linear Regression

HousePriceModel = linear_model.LinearRegression(normalize=True)

#Fitting the Model

HousePriceModel.fit(x_train, y_train)

#Pridicting the House Price

HousePrice_predicted= HousePriceModel.predict(x_test)

#Display the Pridicted value

display(HousePrice_predicted)

```
[28] #Let's divide the dataset into two parts, one for training and other for testing.
     x_train, x_test, y_train, y_test = train_test_split(x, y, train_size=0.33, test_size=0.67, random_state=100)

     #Selecting the Algorithm for the model: Linear Regression
     HousePriceModel = linear_model.LinearRegression(normalize=True)

     #Fitting the Model
     HousePriceModel.fit(x_train, y_train)

     #Pridicting the House Price
     HousePrice_predicted= HousePriceModel.predict(x_test)

     #Display the Pridicted value
     display(HousePrice_predicted)

     array([45.01032238, 36.80889727, 55.28439056, 39.19484954, 52.28076085,
            32.9896596 , 49.36387845, 52.28076085, 52.14144462, 33.43628311,
            34.54622145, 45.10427792, 41.27857979, 30.47830482, 50.17631025,
            38.275791  , 54.51656601, 43.06257175, 33.97904698, 28.44343264,
            12.81333582, 43.59277269, 38.2670058 , 52.58125208, 31.08806928,
            31.96987097, 25.54780597, 41.2316681 , 41.17832718, 40.53009298,
            56.20083367, 37.81927189, 43.61348375, 45.20722049, 29.01501327,
            48.80922473, 37.4501225 , 18.14243029, 48.77727958, 55.06283112,
            45.20370983, 44.30347776, 35.53229929, 35.22990078, 40.70253611,
            45.1729063 , 40.85413609, 31.72019064, 41.20398208, 49.13700039,
            41.32082845, 34.79198245, 40.5687417 , 40.4068103 , 52.14144462,
            46.32024021, 48.77424723, 35.33284335, 49.66569508, 32.88467142,
            39.52107708, 48.93643861, 50.03905348, 36.42348221, 40.36285656,
            47.953739  , 50.24493863, 45.89350431, 38.19072291, 51.37190255,
             7.56351689, 34.0010245 , 45.10427792, 48.91150399, 48.84287561,
            33.91097696, 49.47867004, 35.63571993, 41.04107042, 26.65805061,
            40.75513559, 56.18867925, 49.08936493, 45.21620753, 44.73160981,
            45.02518592, 41.42199219, 47.92905967, 48.09275128, 40.69652612,
            48.40443951, 28.09839338, 41.42199219, 55.35301894, 46.29370083,
            44.6231144 , 44.81930077, 47.23006063, 46.01060422,  7.05908658,
            42.11955552, 44.12821315, 48.93643861, 39.9791896 , 18.64095276,
            32.46428699, 45.09646222, 40.0138975 , 39.91056121, 36.53947224,
            44.05913196, 36.87752565, 45.11326496, 44.75067239, 36.00366388,
            54.45698243, 34.51746893, 32.68856312, 36.67235112, 34.13617992,
            33.32619415, 47.91942481, 19.17185602, 43.98484524, 39.58580432,
            43.25054676, 40.93671487, 43.66767802, 34.52657763, 33.72881649,
            48.35255228, 55.25007637, 45.92511327, 34.72721995, 34.6638344 ,
            55.45596152, 49.01444657, 40.59872136, 49.17663795, 45.37879144,
            19.11672742, 49.00506699, 45.1729063 , 37.25377187, 41.9212661 ,
            32.47312236, 36.13691474, 54.25358887, 33.11526821, 42.60715286,
            42.11874341, 44.02633388, 37.89329799, 35.8838216 , 52.87740728,
```

#Choosing the Graph type

pylab.scatter(HousePrice_predicted,y_test)

#Applying labels

pylab.xlabel('Predicted')

pylab.ylabel('Actual')

```
[29] #Choosing the Graph type
     pylab.scatter(HousePrice_predicted,y_test)

     #Applying labels
     pylab.xlabel('Predicted')
     pylab.ylabel('Actual')
```

Text(0, 0.5, 'Actual')